MW01269074

# THE WORLD'S DEADLIEST INSECTS

## Animal Book of Records
## Children's Animal Books

BABY PROFESSOR
EDUCATION KIDS

Speedy Publishing LLC

40 E. Main St. #1156

Newark, DE 19711

www.speedypublishing.com

Copyright 2017

All Rights reserved. No part of this book may be reproduced or used in any way or form or by any means whether electronic or mechanical, this means that you cannot record or photocopy any material ideas or tips that are provided in this book.

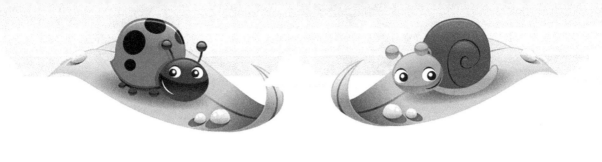

Insects are a lot smaller than people, but they can still be dangerous. Learn about small insects that cause you big problems!

# TINY BUT DANGEROUS

Insects are small and all around us, and most of the time they don't pay any attention to us. They are interested in getting on with their lives. They are born, grow up, have their own babies, and die. Along the way they have to get food and avoid being food for birds, spiders, fish, or other threats.

Colorado Potato Beetle

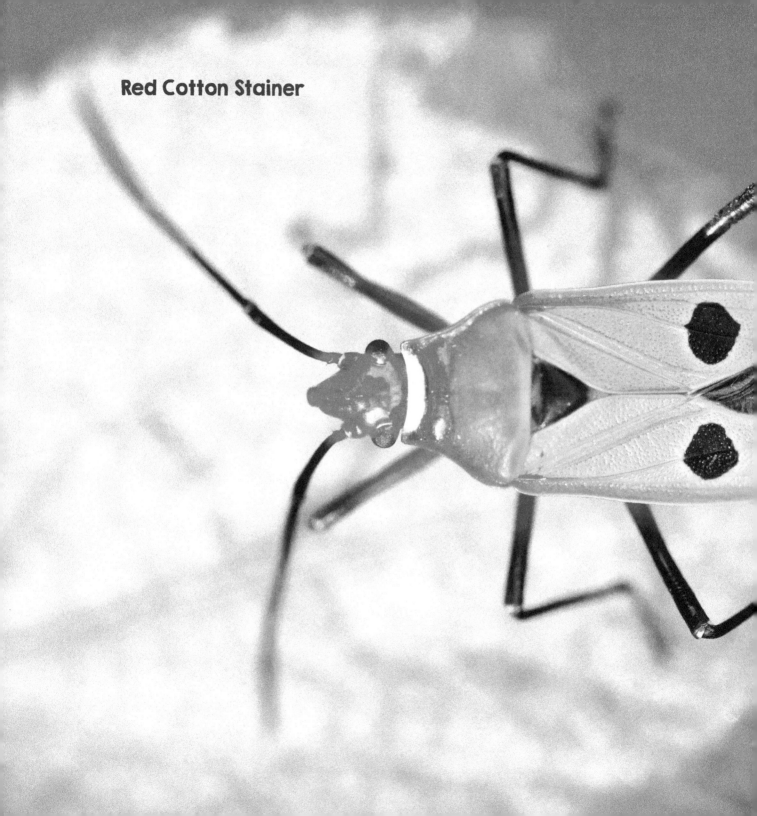

Red Cotton Stainer

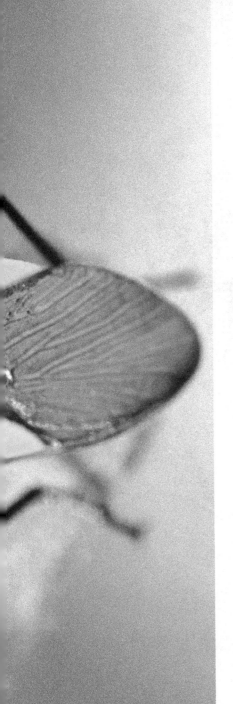

Insect behavior that we find dangerous is often just their way of surviving. When they can, insects will bite us to get blood. Some will try to lay their eggs in us! And if we bother them, many insects will use their stingers, bad smells, or other weapons to try to defend themselves. But maybe it will make that sting on your arm itch less if you remember that the insect that did it was not really trying to hurt you. You mainly just got in its way!

Here are some of the insects that are most dangerous to humans, even if they don't mean to be.

Devil's Coach-Horse Beetle

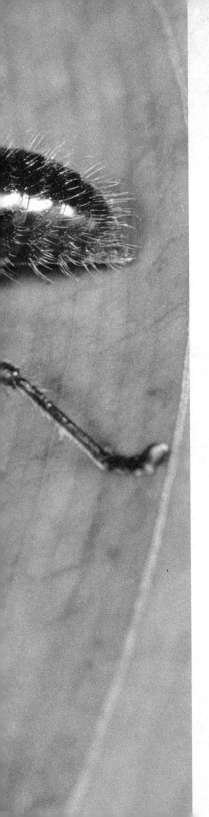

# BULLET ANTS

Bullet ants are the largest type of ant in the world, growing to about one inch long. They live in the rainforests of Central and South America. They get their name because their bite feels like somebody just shot you with a gun! It would take thirty bee stings to match the pain just one bullet ant can cause.

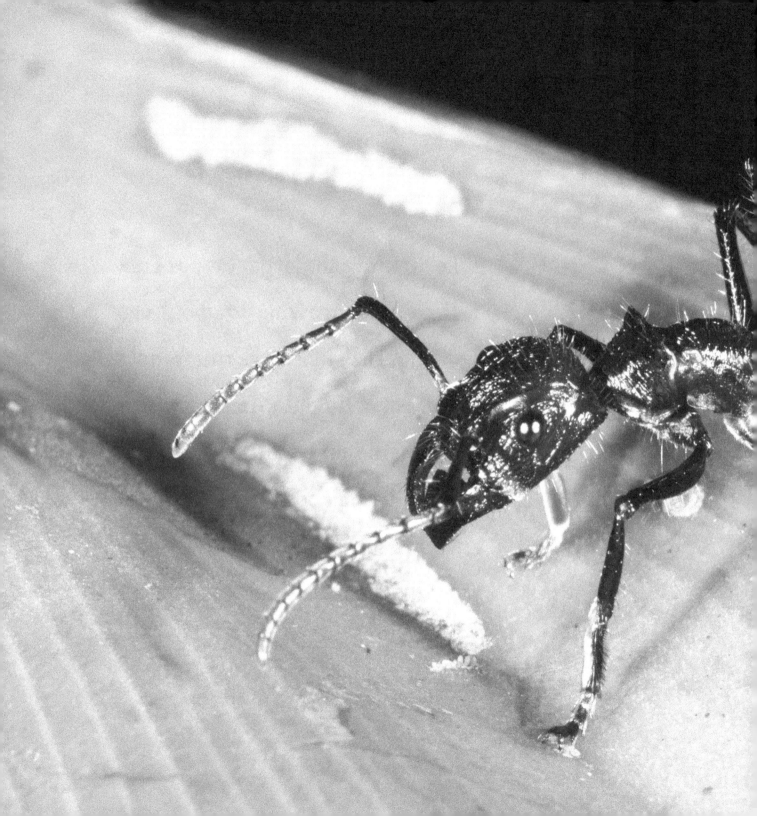

The ants are also called "twenty-four hour ants". That's how long the pain lasts after a bullet ant bites you.

Bullet ants make their nests among the roots of large trees, and live in colonies of hundreds of ants.

When something disturbs their colony, the ants can release a foul smell. If that doesn't drive the intruder away, they are ready to bite!

# BOTFLIES

Botflies mainly live in Central and South America. They lay their eggs under the skin of warm-blooded animals. The eggs hatch into larvae which dig further into the animal and feed on it for about 60 days, until they are ready to emerge as young botflies.

**Horse Botfly**

Botfly

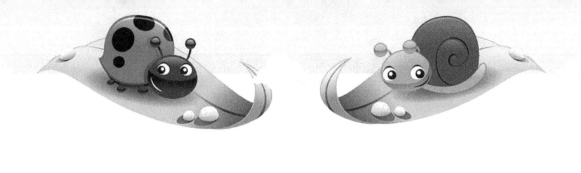

When a botfly chooses a human to carry its eggs, the result can be terrible. Not only can they cause a terrible scar when the new botfly is ready to emerge, they can cause a parasitic infection called "myiasis" that damages the skin.

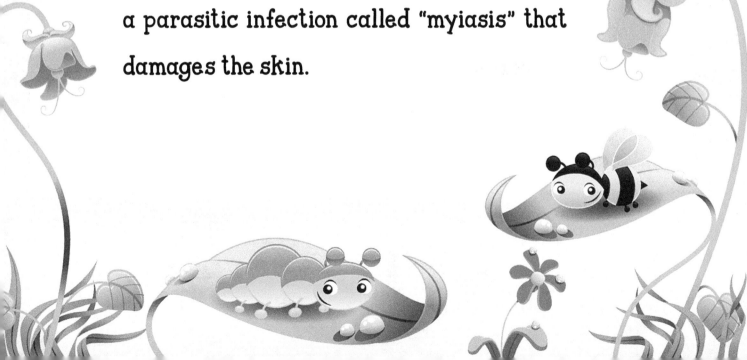

# JAPANESE GIANT HORNETS

The largest hornets in the world live in Japan. They can be two inches long! As many as forty people die every year after being stung by Japanese giant hornets. Their venom tries to dissolve tissues in the body, and often sets off an allergic reaction. Multiple hornet stings over a short period can be more than a person can survive.

Japanese Giant Hornet

Japanese Giant Hornets

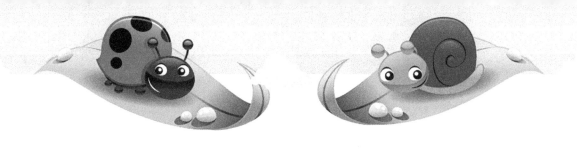

These hornets are very aggressive in defending their colonies, which can hold almost a thousand hornets. Their main target for food is honey bee larvae. They only attack humans when they think we are a threat, but they are very quick to feel threatened!

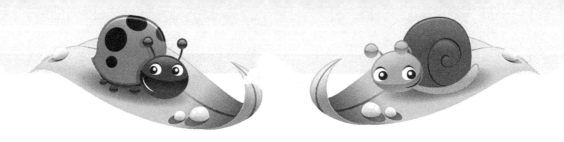

# DISEASE CARRIERS

Some insects are dangerous to us not for what they do directly, but for infections they can deliver. Here are some:

**Mosquito**

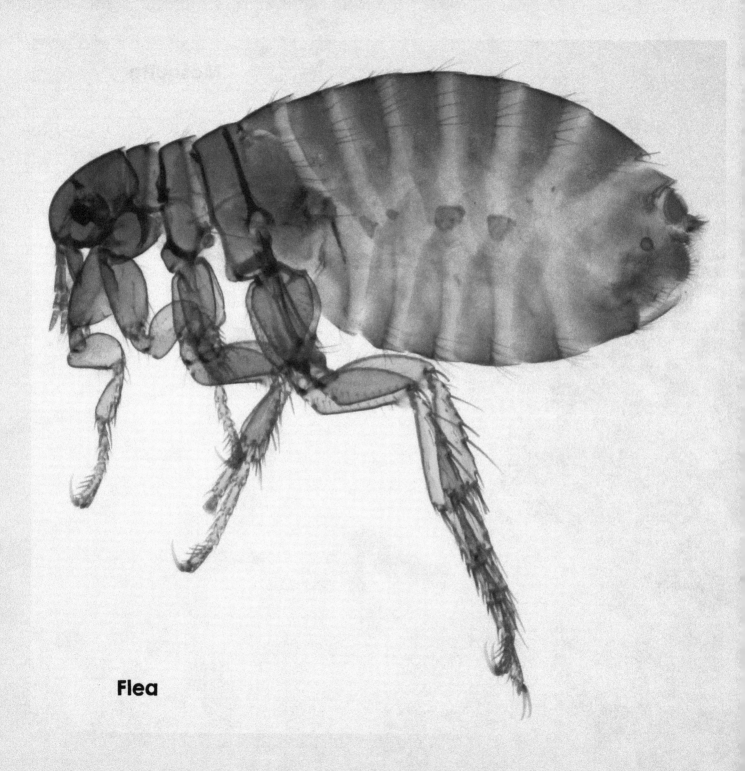

**Flea**

# FLEAS

Fleas are parasites that live on animals of all kinds, including humans. They bite us to drink our blood, and the bites can be itchy. When we scratch the bites, they can become infected and cause a painful rash.

Fleas also can transmit deadly diseases. The "black plague" that killed as much as a third of Europe's population in the Middle Ages came to Europe in rats that traveled in merchant ships. Once in Europe, fleas from the rats bit humans and passed the disease along. Read more about the black plague in the Baby Professor book The Deadliest Diseases in History.

Black Plague

**Kissing Bugs**

# KISSING BUGS

Kissing bugs live on the blood of warm-blooded animals. They get their name from the way they like to bite around the lips of humans while we are asleep. This leaves an embarrassing rash of small bites in the morning. Worse than the rash is the parasite that the kissing bug leaves in the bite wound. More than 12,000 people die every year from the effect of this parasite.

Although the kissing bug's range includes Central America, Mexico, and the southern United States, it is mainly active in homes that are in poor repair, or that have dirt floors. This means that poor, rural people are more likely to suffer from the disease the kissing bug brings than people who live in modern houses or in cities.

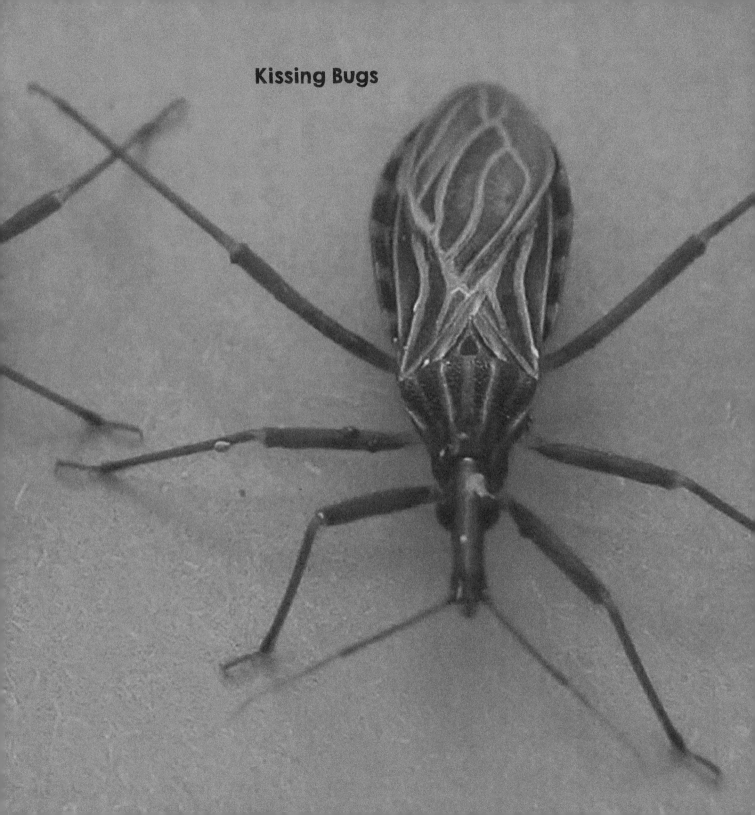

Kissing Bugs

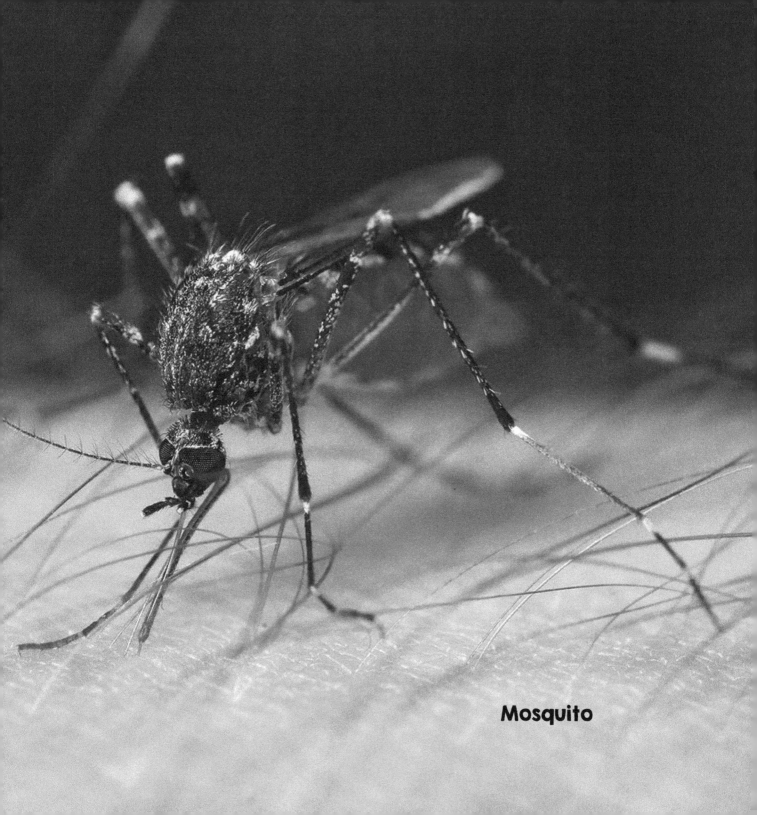

Mosquito

# MOSQUITOES

The most dangerous insect to humans is the mosquito. It is not just an annoying pest at your picnic. Over one million people a year die from diseases that mosquitoes spread, like malaria. When the mosquito bites your arm, it can transmit parasites or germs it picked up from another person or an animal. There are over five hundred million new cases of malaria every year, most of them caused by mosquito bites!

Mosquitoes can also transmit dengue and yellow fever, West Nile virus, and even encephalitis!

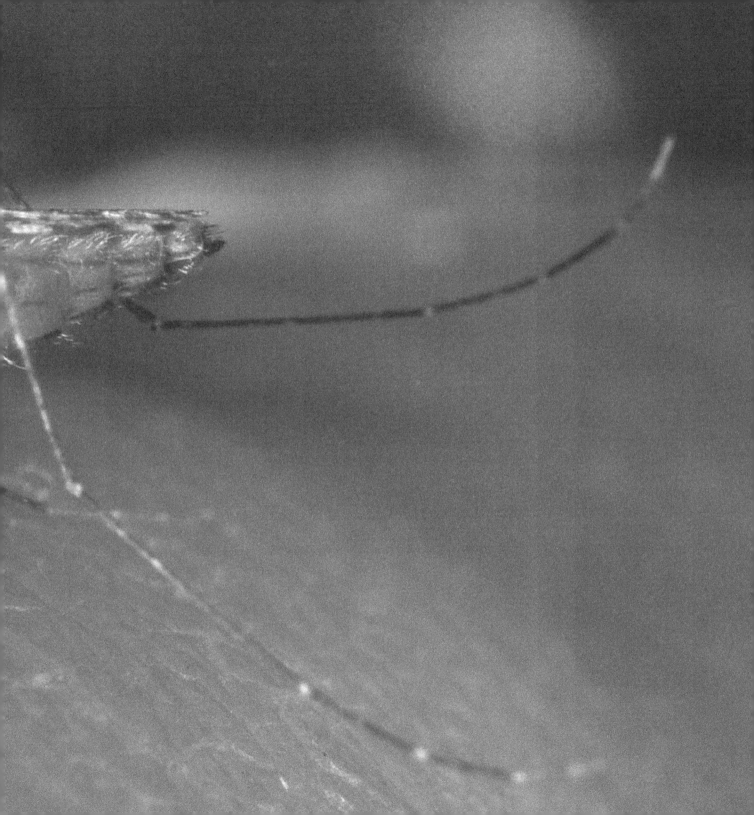

Tsetse Fly

# TSETSE FLIES

The tsetse fly is a plague in Africa. It lives on the blood of warm-blooded animals, and injects a nasty poison each time it takes a drink. Over half a million people die from tsetse fly attacks every year, and million suffer from diseases like sleeping sickness that the fly transmits.

# SWARMS OF DANGER

Many insects work together in colonies or hives. Most of the time they get on about their business of gathering food and raising babies. However, sometimes, when what they want to do bumps into human activity, it can be a problem for the humans!

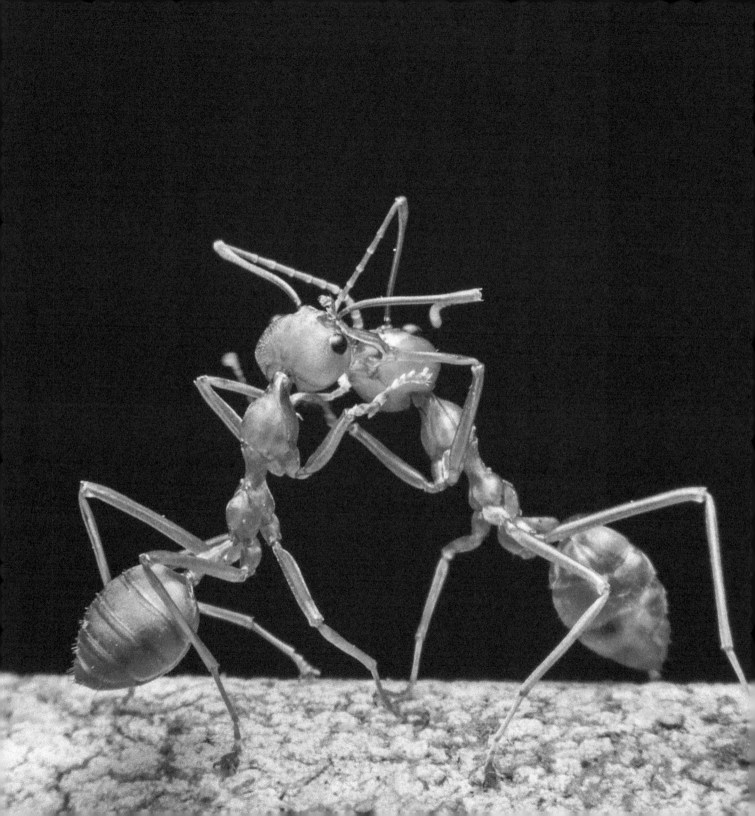

# FIRE ANTS

Most of the 285 fire ant species are not a threat to humans. However, red fire ants can be a real problem in the United States, China, Australia, and some other countries. They deliver a painful bite with venom that can cause a wound that takes weeks to heal. This can lead to skin problems or possibly-deadly allergic reactions.

The real problem is that, when they are threatened, fire ants attack as a group of tens or hundreds of ants. That many bites can actually kill a person!

Honey Bee

# KILLER BEES

Africanized honey bees, or "killer bees", live in colonies of as many as one hundred thousand members, from Brazil as far north as the southern United States. They are very aggressive and persistent: if a human or animal bothers their colony, they attack and may continue to follow their target for as much as a mile.

When killer bees attack people, they aim at the face and eyes. No one sting is dangerous, but the bees tend to attack in large groups.

Honey Bee

Driver Ant

# DRIVER ANTS

A driver ant colony may have more than twenty million members. They live mainly in East Africa and parts of Asia. When food supplies run low around their colony, the driver ants move in a long column in search of food. They will eat anything they run into, both plants and animals, and even elephants run away from driver ants that are on the move.

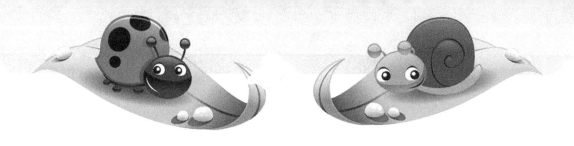

If driver ants attack a person, they can cause serious damage with hundreds of painful bites. On the other hand, when they pass through a village, driver ants can kill off snakes, rats, and other pests and actually leave the village in better shape than it was before they arrived!

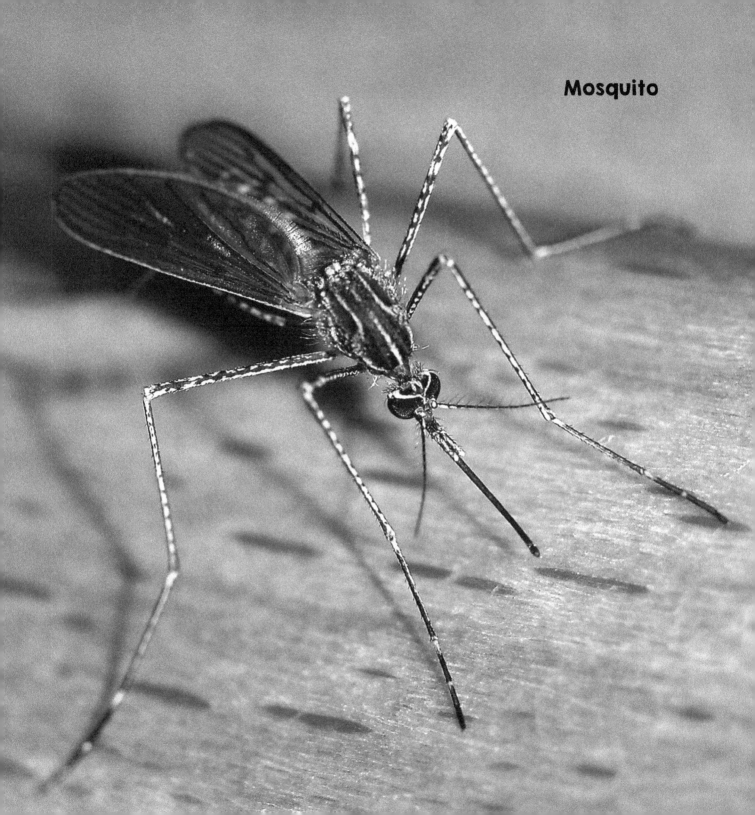

Mosquito

# DEALING WITH
# DANGEROUS INSECTS

There are some simple steps you can take to reduce the chance that dangerous insects will harm you.

- ✎ Protect yourself. If you are going to be outdoors in an area or at a time of day when biting insects are active, wear appropriate clothing and use insect repellent.

- ✎ Check yourself. Insects like ticks can travel on your body for a while before deciding where to bite.

- ✎ Check for bites. If you have a bite that continues to be painful or look red or swollen over several days, visit your doctor to see what's up.

- ✎ Don't look for trouble. If you see a beehive, or are visiting a country where driver ants may be on the move, don't go closer to check it out. The insects may see you as a threat, or as lunch!

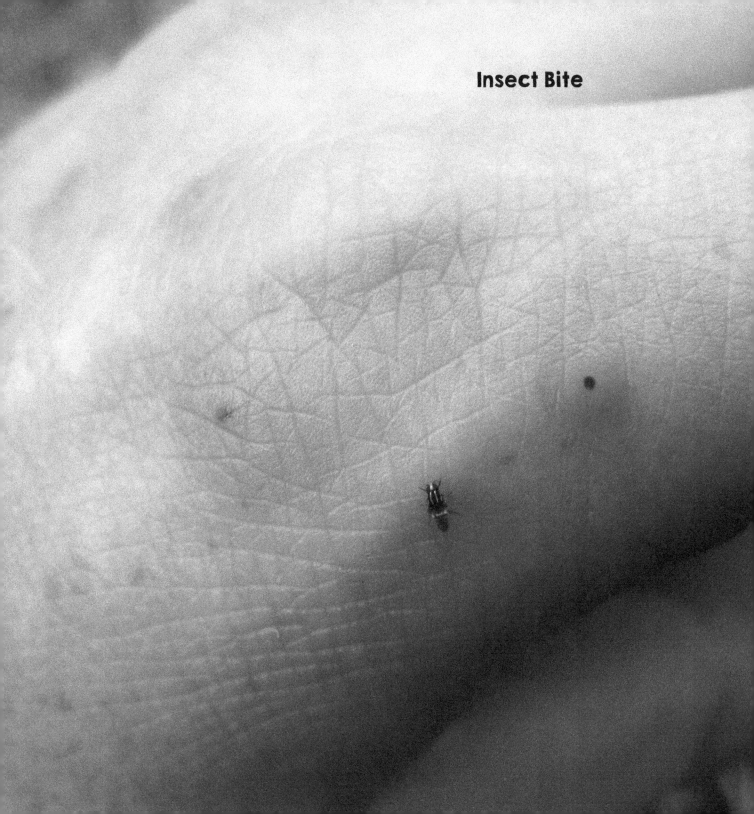

**Insect Bite**

Children under five years old, pregnant women, people over 65 years old, and people with health problems or severe allergies have to be especially careful. Insects are small, but they can pack a punch!

# OTHER TINY DANGERS

You may be saying, "Hey! Where's the black widow spider?" They are dangerous, too; but spiders are arachnids, not insects. Learn about how they differ in the Baby Professor book Insects and Arachnids, and read about air-borne insects in Discovering the Flying Insects.

Black Widow

Visit

**BABY PROFESSOR**
EDUCATION KIDS

# www.BabyProfessorBooks.com

to download Free Baby Professor eBooks
and view our catalog of new and exciting
Children's Books

CPSIA information can be obtained
at www.ICGtesting.com
Printed in the USA
BVHW021320161222
654327BV00011B/942